Romantic Comedies
of
Online Dating

ChaCha McKnight

Disclaimer:

I have tried to recreate events, locales and conversations from my memories of them. In order to maintain their anonymity in some instances I have changed the names of individuals and places, I may have changed some identifying characteristics and details such as physical properties, occupations and places of residence.

ISBN-10: 0692243461
ISBN-13: 978-06922434-6-6

ChaChaMcKnight@gmail.com

Edited by:
Jennifer-Crystal Johnson
www.JenniferCrytalJohnson.com

Table of Contents

Dedication

To my friends, P. Wilson & B. Hoke; without these two amazing women I wouldn't have had the courage to write about my crazy online dating experiences.

Acknowledgements

A special thanks to my family. Words cannot express how grateful I am to my mother for all of the sacrifices that she's made on my behalf. Her prayers for me were what sustained me thus far.

I would also like to thank my daughter, Tatiana, who supported me in my writing, and incented me to strive towards my goal.

Finally, I would like express appreciation to my beloved sister, Terry, who kept me calm when I had sleepless nights and was always my support in the moments when there was no one to answer my queries.

Introduction

Although I wrote this book to share my crazy, unbelievable experiences, there is a serious side I want women and men to consider when dating online. Be sure to check people out before meeting face to face; really get to know them by using public places for a while and don't allow them to know where you live until you are sure about their character.

Chapter One

My first experience with internet dating was a doozy, to say the least. I'll refrain from mentioning specific dating sites in order not to diminish their brand, utility, and value, because the sites have nothing to do with *my* bizarre experiences. I've heard rumors that some folks have found true love on there; rumors seldom lean on the side of facts, though. Enough said.

My first experience was with a man I met online who had a wonderful profile that seemed to meet all of my high requirements; plus, his photographs made my mouth and other intimate areas water. We promptly set up an appointment and, when we did meet at a local restaurant, he was much older than his picture portrayed him to be, not to mention much heavier, too. Ugh!

Of course, I got the hell out of there. My exit happened quite fortuitously; I had run into a friend of mine when I got to the restaurant and told her I was there to meet a guy but I wasn't sure what he looked like. She laughed and jokingly said to me, "Well, if he isn't what you want let me know by giving me the scratch-your-head sign and I will call your cell saying that you're needed at home immediately."

This man was a total fraud! He was not only much older and heavier than he represented in his profile, he was also a grandpa and was totally into active grand-parenting. Now, if that's fine for you, that's alright; but it's not so for me! So, needless to say,

I scratched my head, my girl called my cell, and I got the hell out of there.

Crazy as that story was, that was one of my mildest experiences; you would have thought I would learn my first lesson (for free, too), but nope, I didn't, and my stubborn adventure would cost me a lot of hard-earned money, time, and heartache.

Chapter Two

The next man I met actually flew to California to meet me and turned out to be everything I *didn't* want. I met up with him for a Christmas dinner somewhere in the ritzy area of Blackhawk, California. During dinner I grew very bored with our conversation, and although he came bearing gifts and I had nary for him, I politely excused myself and ran out the back door, never to be seen or heard from again and leaving the gifts behind.

You guessed it... he blew up my cell, cussing me out, and maybe I should have told him I wasn't interested, but maybe he should have been honest about his height and looks, too, and I wouldn't have responded like that. People shouldn't lie on those sites because you will actually meet in person, and virtual lies will be unscreened. Stop lying!

Lies, however, have no gender. I hear from my male friends that women put up pictures from when they were younger and much thinner. Speaking of which, I once drove one of my male friends to meet a lady he met on some dating site. His verification method was way smarter than mine: he said to circle around the parking lot and, if she didn't look anything like her picture, he wanted me to just drive off.

Chapter Three

I moved to Minnesota, and as new residents are wont to feel, I was lonely. So I got on the Internet again, hoping I would find love via the net *this* time. Well, I was fooled again, like so many times before. I met this guy from St. Thomas Islands and was so taken by him that I flew out there not knowing what I was walking into.

He came out to meet me at the airport and, of course, as the now all-too-familiar pattern goes, he looked nothing like his picture! It's such an optical fraud how people can look bigger, stronger, and taller in pictures. This guy had a floating eye, was shorter than me, and not to mention he wasn't muscular like his pictures made him out to be. I guess he Photo-shopped his pictures or something because that sure wasn't the same guy. Well… there was nothing I could do but make the best of it; after all, I was miles and hard-earned-air-ticket-cash away from the cold winter of Minnesota and now banked on a tropical island with some ugly, cross-eyed man. I asked him to show me around all three islands and it was fun once I got past his fucking eyes crossing every which way. I tried not to stare at him because I didn't want him to think I noticed his eyes floating all over the damn place… I was getting dizzy just looking at him. I finally relaxed and was able to move on with my trip.

My villa was so not-American-4-star standard; I had one room with stuff piled up in a corner with a sheet covering it. Only God knows what was under those sheets; I didn't dare look since it was none of my business. My bed was so high up that if I got up in the middle of the night, I would hit the ceiling, fall out of bed, and fall into the bathroom. I always slept light in fear of falling down the stairs. The bed was something like this, but not as nice. At least here you can sit up; I had to roll out of bed each and every time.

In the morning, Floating-eyes came to pick me up and take me around all three islands, and for the most part, it was fun tasting all the foods and learning the culture. I stood out like a rose in the middle of winter; the natives treated me like I was some sort of celebrity or something and the men were very aggressive, pulling and tugging my arms, hands, and clothes. I toured all three islands, and it was so orgasmically beautiful. When it came time for intimacy, so he thought anyway, I was able to avoid having sex with him by saying I was on my period. I tell ya, I would have cut myself and showed him blood rather than to have that cat touch me. Whew! Thank God he was one of those men who don't like having sex with a woman during that time of month.

(Hahaha, fooled ya!)

This fool really thought I was going to marry his ass! Really! What drugs was he on? The only thing he had going for himself was his business, which was successful, and everybody knew him. With me on his arm, it made him the man of the year. Yuck! He went on and on about me running his business, really trying to dangle the carrot in front of me. I believe his business was construction. I just couldn't get past the floating eyes that kept making me dizzy! On top of that he was shorter than me; that was a turn off to me. I am tall and I love tall men. If I wore heels around Floating-eyes, he would have looked more like a child standing next to me, not a mate, and I just can't have that. I have a right to like what I want and he just wasn't it. Next!

I had a great time on all three of the islands, and when it came time for me to leave, I left with grace, my ass untouched and my middle finger up in the air. I had plans never to return to see Floating-eyes' black ass again.

Chapter Four

Once I got back to my ice-cold home in Minnesota, I went back to the computer to torture myself some more by hitting the net again. There was no such thing as Skype yet, so you pretty much had to take folks' word about who they were.

This time, my attention was caught by a beautiful, tall, chocolate-cream colored man who I thought was living in Charlotte, NC at the time… but that turned out to be another lie. Now, keep in mind this is before the Western Union African schemes were widely known. Yep, I was one of the first victims of that crap. This brother sent me pictures of his so-called house on the inside and out, cars… nothing too fancy so it was easy to believe; but you could see the brother had it going on. I took the bait and I was in for a ride.

We corresponded a lot every day throughout the day, so I could tell he was into me and I was definitely into him. All was going well between us until he hit me with the, "I am stranded and I need money to get home," bullshit. I questioned it, but I investigated his house in NC, his work, and all that checked out. I didn't have any reason to feel like I was being set up for some crap.

He said he needed a ticket home; it was expensive, something like $1300.00. I told him to call me – no more emails. Well, he called and his voice didn't match his look, but I hear that about myself so I didn't put a lot of weight on it. When he did call, he sounded like Mike Tyson and I was shocked. I didn't like that type of voice; it wasn't making me horny at all, but I had to stop being so damn picky. So, this cat said if I didn't get him out of there the police were going to hurt him and I was like damn, don't put that stress on me and I don't even know you really; but having the heart I do, I said ok, I will get the ticket.

I asked, "How much do you need?" You would think that this guy would have been happy, but he wanted me to send it to him via Western Union. We got into it over doing it that way verses me just purchasing it for him, and now I had red flags going up. What was this guy up to? But my mind and body wanted this tall chocolate glass of milk, so I was going to do whatever it took to get him. When I tell you this man was good with his words, I mean he was so good he could have sold me silver and told me it was diamonds and I would have believed him. My judgment was clouded with envisioning us rolling around on the bed making passionate love over and over again. All of his pictures were so soft, sexy, and professional at the same time and I wanted him; not to mention he was blessed, if you know what I mean.

Alas, the truth came out three days later, but not before I sent that damn money for his so-called ticket! Ugh! Fuck me! I should have known that his pictures were phony... they were just too perfect, almost model-like.

By day four, he called me to say he was unable to come back because he missed his flight. I just looked at the phone in embarrassment. I couldn't believe a smart woman like myself could be taken for such a cheap ass ride and schemed out of so much money. But then again, it's happened, and I wasn't going to beat myself up about it anymore. Well, he had his airbrushed photos, his lies, and now my money, and that was that. Nothing I could do about it. I called Western Union and, at that time, they had no clue about these types of scams, so I was just out of luck.

The balls of some people... this fool had the nerve to try to continue communicating with me, thinking he could get more money out of me. The nerve! It's funny how every now and then he tried to communicate with me by using someone else's photo; but I knew how he talked and typed, so he couldn't fool me again. Once beaten, twice armed. Get the fuck outta here!

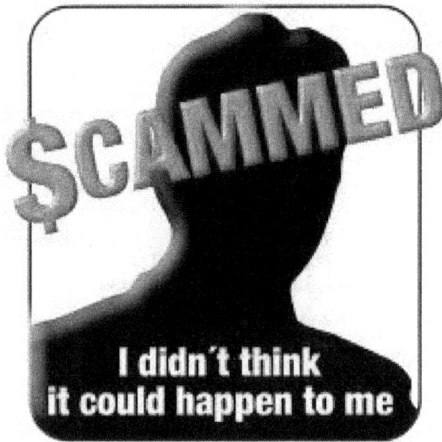

SCAMMED

I didn't think it could happen to me

Chapter Five

Now, unbelievably, there's more. Talk about an unrepentant optimist. The next one was a tad bit closer to home as he resided in Canada. The point of attraction was that we had mutual interests: music, plain and simple, or at least so I thought. Apparently nothing is simple when it comes to me.

The time came to meet this deep-voiced, sexy man behind the music. When I arrived at the airport, true to my aura, some man came up to me to carry my bags all the way to the arrival's lounge where my artist associate would be waiting for me. As we walked in, a man just materialized out of nowhere and literally took my breath away, for standing before me was my artist, who, for once throughout my internet dating life, looked everything like his photo, plus he was slender and taller than me. I breathed a sigh of relief and had to make a grand entrance by sashaying into his open arms.

The artist stood there in amazement as I got closer and closer to him, with my luggage carrier walking like a servant behind me. When I got within arm's length he smiled ear to ear and asked me, "Who is this guy with you?" I smiled and said, "I don't know, he just wanted to carry my bags for me." As we went to exit the airport, I was amazed at the beauty of it. There's so much to see in Toronto; it's an amazing place... the people, the culture, and just the entire attitude is far different than here in the United

States. My experience was a good one; everyone was so nice to me.

Well, we finally got to my hotel room; I showered, changed, and came down to the lobby. I looked around and there he was in front of the hotel, waiting for me in this Jaguar knock-off. He looked sexy in it, that's for sure. I put a smile on my face and walked over to the car. He got out to open the door for me. I got in, crossed my legs (which looked better than usual because I had on fishnet pantyhose with sexy high heels; I knew that would fuck his ass up), and we drove to the venue where he was to perform. I could see him cutting his eyes over at my legs and smiling at me. As good as he looked, I didn't care; I wanted to tease him.

We arrived at the venue and, like a gentleman, he got out and opened the door for me and I followed him and his musical partner to the back door of the venue. The back door guard let us in and we walked through this smoky place with other acts getting ready to perform. There were also vendors cooking in huge pots; I later learned it was Trinidadian food and it smelled so darn good. I was escorted to the first row, where friends and family sit to watch the artists perform. Screaming began, the lights went out, and there was an act before my artist was to perform, so it was all good. I was damn tired but I jammed on. All of the acts were good, but I was waiting on the tall thin one. Once the group came out, all the girls stared screaming and at that point I knew I wanted to manage these guys. Canada knew who they were, but I wanted the rest of the world to know them as well. My jaw fell to the floor when I heard their music, dollar signs flashing across my eyes. I had the money and they had the talent; I wanted to work with them and see where this could go.

When we left, we went to the musical partner's house to discuss what I could do for them. Both of them were very excited because I didn't just talk the talk; I got folks on the phone to back up my claims, and unfortunately, I can't mention their names. I can say that, as soon I got back to Minnesota, I was able to retain legal services from a famous entertainment attorney who once had a client I am very fond of in the music industry. I had to become their manager before someone else grabbed them.

This music was very different; these guys called it "rapso," which is like the Caribbean's version of R&B music. The two together were so different. I opened up my home to both of them and paid for them both to come to the States and reside with me while working on their CD. I pulled them aside and gave them the low down of the business, told them not to get anyone pregnant and not to have any relationships until they're established artists. Having a relationship early in the game will only cloud your creative thinking.

Finally, I was happy! We were winning every competition there is; I even flew them to Vegas and they won on a TV show. These guys were on fire and people were taking notice, and I was right there to get them on the map. After winning the TV competition, the tall thin one and I retreated to a room where he just sat in front of the window, taking in all of the good fortune. I told him I was going to get some air, so I went over to the other artist's room to check on him. As I walked in, he was very much involved in oral sex with an associate of mine. I picked my jaw up and quickly turned around and left. I waited until they were done with whatever they were doing to move on to our next adventure to celebrate the group winning the on the TV show.

I have travelled to Canada many times and mostly stayed in a hotel, all except this one time when the artist asked me to spend the night at his house. I thought I was going to get busy with this cutie pie... wrong! I was put in a guest room with an air mattress and he closed the door. My jaw dropped, but I turned over and went to sleep. I felt I was getting mixed messages: did he like me or did he just want me to help his career have an American push, which he made indirect allusions to? I wanted both, damn it!

I must admit here that I do have a huge personality which intimidates most men. I am gifted with brains, beauty, confidence, et al, which has made many a man wonder what in the world I would need him for; this turns the tables on me at times. So here I was, in need of being needed for something totally not on my menu. He ended up coming with me to America and occupied my spare room. I didn't mind at that time.

Chapter Six

Another damn artist contacted me via email, this time a rock and roll guitar player. He played guitar for a famous artist I love and admire. When this guitarist played a well-known song for me, I melted. The big turn off with this one was how filthy he kept his home; cigarettes everywhere, and I hate that! The shower curtain was mildewed, yuck!

I still had the other artist at my home, but I felt it was my home so I would do what I wanted. Besides, the first artist kept sending mixed messages and I was tired of it. I actually invited the new artist to my home to pick me up, but his car conked out in my driveway, so he begged to spend the night. To me that was as bad as running out of gas. I knew that was a bunch of crap but deliberately fell for it anyway, and of course I wanted his piece of junk of a car out of my driveway. Well, I guess I thought I was the Mack since I had one guy living in with me (staying in my spare room) and my new friend in the bedroom with me, eating my candy up! Bold right.

Well, lo and behold, no sooner had we entered my room when artist number one came walking in, stood in the doorway taking in what he was seeing, and proceeded to ask what the hell was going on. I looked up, in shock at being walked in on, but didn't go off. I asked him to just leave my room and he did, but by now the other artist was upset and uncomfortable saying that he wanted to fight the other guy and I should have warned him. I did mention I had someone living with me I dated but it didn't work out, so we were roommates. I guess the artist had feelings for me after all. My reasoning and attitude was, well, you had a chance to be with me and passed it up to live off of me instead, so naturally I am giving someone else a chance. Artist number two had his own place, so we went there and damn, need I remind you, that house was a hot mess! OMG! I also discovered that his morning breath mixed with coffee and cigarettes smelled like hot manure on fire! But man, when he played that guitar I melted and forgot all about his filthy morning breath and horrible housekeeping.

He was so sexy on stage; the way he stroked that guitar and made those sexy O-faces was such a turn on. As for his life behind the curtain, that was another story. If those groupies knew what I knew, they would head for the hills and never look back. We didn't work out because I couldn't deal with baby mama drama groupies and his nasty habits. With me being a clean freak, it wouldn't work out. The rock and roll life wasn't for me, period, so I dumped him. The guitar artist who shall remain nameless did say he would give it all up to be with me, but for some reason or another, I just wasn't feeling him, besides what I have already mentioned before. Although it was sweet, I didn't want him to give up music and I wasn't in love with him. Goodbye, guitar man... on to the next adventure.

Chapter Seven

I decided to try this popular black dating site, and what a joke; need I say more? Along came another freaking weirdo who had a semi-famous father. I really can't mention this man's name because his father is a heavyweight in politics, but we will call him Sneaky.

So, Sneaky was a chip off the old block. He was well-groomed, carried himself in a nice, fashionable way; he could spend money on me without blinking or whining about it like a few have before him. Sneaky had his act together. He owned a few businesses and wasn't married... hmmm, I wondered why. I was about to find out. What I was in for... you can't make this crap up.

Sneaky only came to visit me, and when he did, he wined and dined me all over the place. One drawback was that I had never been to his house; not once in the year or two we dated. He even put a down payment on a house for me and I made the mortgage payments. I kept my suspicions to myself since he was doing so much for me. Sneaky was so into me that he financed my fashion line. I could tell he got the money from his dad because the one time I was allowed to speak to him, I was coached on what to say and not to mention we were an item, so that was strange. By now I was convinced he was married, but why would he introduce me to his son? That was a big question mark, since the kid could go back and tell his mom.

I kept quiet because I didn't want to push too hard. I was worried he would back off if his secret came out. We traveled to the islands, made love under the stars, and danced the night away. It amazed me that a man could be so good to me. If I was upset about something, he didn't yell, scream, or get defensive; he just talked our problems out. I was thinking, *what a catch... now if I could just get to his secret.*

While traveling, if I even glanced at something in a store window he would ask me if I wanted it and buy it without the blink of an eye. Man, am I spoiled or what? Too good to be true? Yep, he was Sneaky... he had weird sexual habits, wearing two to three rubbers and then asking for oral sex with them on. Can you imagine having oral sex on a balloon? Not exactly my idea of a romantic evening. I declined by saying I don't perform oral sex, and to be honest, I really don't like to unless we are in a monogamous relationship. I asked him to perform oral sex on me and he wouldn't, claiming he has mysophobia. I understood that because I didn't like the exchange of bodily fluids at one time myself, so I let it go. Oral sex in our relationship was out of the question, and I was fine with that.

As Sneaky and I grew closer, I often wondered if he was married, but as it turned out, that wasn't his reason for keeping me away from his inner circle. He was just eccentric like that, but at the same time, he was very sneaky about how he did things and that was always a red flag... but I continued with the strange relationship. After a few years of this crazy life, I decided to let it go. Sneaky wanted to call the shots, and that worked for a while, but I got tired of spending holidays alone, so I just broke it off... or at least I thought it would be that easy.

I showed Sneaky I was serious by moving to back to California and purchasing a wonderful 2800 sq. ft. home outside of Tracy. He flew out to come see me as often as he could, but it wasn't the same. What I wanted he just couldn't give me. I asked him one more time to move in with me and he declined, so I had to cut him off yet again.

I got a butt-dial call from him one day... I could hear him telling someone how he has a beautiful Afro-Puerto Rican girlfriend that he loves but will not commit to. I heard enough, hung up, and called him back and told him what I heard... of course he denied everything. Ugh! How easily he lied to me was jaw-dropping. I was so done with his ass! Too much work for me. I thought that was the end of Sneaky, at least as a lover and possible mate.

The economy dropped and I had to move out of my beautiful home and back to Georgia where the cost of living was much cheaper. I had to call upon Sneaky for help, but as a friend, so Sneaky found me a beautiful home in Alpharetta. As usual,

Sneaky had such exquisite taste I never even had to question what the house looked like. I proceeded with my move to Georgia. I was young, so getting in the car and driving across country was nothing to me. The movers came and picked up my stuff, and off I was to the dirty south. Once we arrived, I was so pleased with the house Sneaky picked out for me! The front living area had a huge window looking at baby mansions, a community pool, and friendly neighbors... so friendly that my next-door neighbor brought cookies and a welcome gift over to the house. I never had that before; coming from Cali, most keep to themselves.

Sneaky bought groceries and other necessities while we waited for the movers to arrive in the next day or so. I reminded him we are no longer an item and not to expect anything more from me than a thank you, period. Well, once I got all moved in and settled, I started going out to local hangouts for a drink and met the next one.

This caramel-skinned man really caught my eye. He sent a drink to my table, and like a gentleman, he came over to introduce himself. I knew he was watching me for a while, probably making sure I was alone before sending a drink. When he came over to sit down, he started staring at me like he hadn't seen a pretty girl before. He then asked what I was mixed with and I told him Puerto Rican and African with a dash of Asian; I paused and smiled. He looked at me and said he wanted to call my mother and thank her; I giggled and we moved on from that subject.

As we sat there in the well-known franchise restaurant, people started coming up to this guy and asking for autographs. I didn't think anything of it because I have been around many celebrities in the past, but I didn't know who he was so I started thinking he had to be in the limelight in an area I have no interest in. Come to think about it, I never caught his first and last name; we just started talking. He later told me his name and looked at me like I was supposed to know who the hell he was…. Well, I didn't, and he was surprised.

I didn't ask and he didn't mention what he did for a living, so we continued to talk a while until my butt hurt from sitting. I stood up to stretch my legs and give my rear a break, and he excused himself to go to the restroom. While he was gone, the bartender gave me a look as though I caught myself a huge fish. I still had no clue who this guy was, nor did I care; I just wanted a man in my life and that turned out to be extremely hard to find.

I was told later who this cat was, but I was unimpressed. I continued to act as thought I didn't have a clue in front of him. I was sure he had many women chasing him and I wasn't going to be one of them; he would have to chase me if he wanted a real person in his life. I am going to call this one Baseball, and you can take what you want from that.

Baseball and I started dating a bit; nothing heavy, just every now and then. All was well until he came to my house to pick me up for a date. I usually met him somewhere, but this time he came to pick me up. He rang my door bell and I invited him in; all he could talk about was how damn small my house was and how big his was! I had to take a step back for a minute. The house Sneaky picked out for me had mansions all around it and mine was a good size, too; a 3500 square foot home isn't bad. Oh, but Mr. Baseball bragged about his 10,000 square foot home in Buckhead and that pissed me off. And what a turn-off! But I just smiled and thought to myself, well then, dumbass, buy me what you feel I should be living in or shut the hell up! We went out in a (of course) custom Porsche that kind of looked like this one but white.

Well, while we drove around town in his flashy car, he let me know how expensive it was by telling me it had this and that. I started to yawn inside and daydream about other stuff. I was in no shape or form interested in what this guy had to say about his damn car. We had our date and he brought me home and started talking about my "puny" house again. I just about lost it, but instead I responded by asking if he wanted me to fix him a drink. While inside I wanted to punch him and kick his ass out.

We chatted over a drink and he said it again about my house! *Ok, now he's going to get it.* I said, "If you don't like my house, buy me a 10,000 square foot home like yours and that way you won't be able to complain about it again!" To my surprise, he said, "Sweetie, you play your cards right you will be moving in with me." This guy was so full of himself I couldn't stand it. He hadn't come across a person like me who said no or told him off like I did, and the more I did it, the more he kept coming by to my house, each time in a different car. The next time he came

by in a Range Rover sort of like this one.

I was bored, so I went with him to some over-priced restaurant. The more you pay, the less food you get, right? When the food was served, I asked the waiter where my salad was and he pointed to my plate… my jaw dropped. We had good conversation this time and the groupies didn't bother us at this restaurant. I guess he could tell I wasn't impressed. He started to tell me all about himself, everything but what he did for a living, and I was cool with that because his head was big enough and I wasn't going to inflate it any more than it already was. He told me about his ex and kids. I thought to myself, *oh, this cat is looking for a baby mama*, and I wasn't down for raising small kids since mine were grown and damn near grown. I had it in my mind to travel and enjoy life, not raise more kids.

Baseball was loaded and had many women after him, so I asked, "Why me?" He said I was what he wanted and needed in his life. I sat there in disbelief, wondering if that was the truth or not. Baseball took me home. I knew he went on tour and I told him that I couldn't deal with him and his lifestyle, and that was the end of that.

All through my lovely adventures, Sneaky was still in the background waiting for me to fail so he could come running to my rescue. I did get in touch with him when I was bored between dating. Sex was out of the question, though; I told him there would be none of that and I meant it.

I was still living in the house that Sneaky found for me in Alpharetta, but I was paying the bills. I met another cat online and this one was some high profile IT guy. We will call him Washington. Washington was a nerd all the way; he had it all but the glasses with tape wrapped around the bridge. We were totally different, but I am always game to try something different; plus, this guy was built like a football player. Most thought he was a retired player and he was very good-looking. I was waiting for the flaw to show and it didn't take long for it to come out.

Washington was so sweet and attentive to all my needs and wants, I was in heaven for the moment. I lived in Georgia and Washington lived in Maryland but flew down every weekend to be with little ole me. I felt so special to have a man that called me all the time and flew down to see me every week; I was hooked! His good looks didn't hurt, either.

Washington didn't hide anything from me like Sneaky did. I was able to fly up to his house and he put me up in the best hotel around. He treated me like he really wanted a good woman in his life. Although he didn't hide anything from me on the top level, of course there are other levels, but let me finish the good stuff first.

Washington took me all around Washington, DC showing me all the tourist sites, eating at all of his favorite restaurants, and enjoying the beaches. All was good and then he asked me to take things to the next level by introducing me to his family. Now we were getting somewhere! Sneaky never did that, so I felt special.

I met his evil has-been-opera-singer sister, his drama queen mother, and his dad, who was cool… and his son, a spoiled ass brat who tried to vacuum up my cat. I haven't liked that kid since.

The mean has-been-opera-singer sister decided to look me up and down and question me like I was on the witness stand. I sure didn't like that. It hit me really fast: this bitch was jealous of me. She always asked why I wore this or that and I finally responded by saying, "Because I can!"

Washington's son was the only child and he looked at me as a threat, so in his mind, I had to go. The mother also looked at me as a threat. Well, little lady, we would see about that. Washington was pleased about how I handled myself with his evil family. He knew they were mean. Heck, they ran off a few of his past lady friends, but I am different. It was going to take more than evil looks to get rid of my ass! What I didn't know was that all of these mean people lived with him in his house and he wanted to add me to the mix. We needed to talk about that crap.

Washington was very interesting. He desperately needed approval from his family about who he was in a relationship with, so I tried to be nice to evil folks who went out of their way to be mean to me. Well, Sunday came and I flew back to Georgia – first class, I might add – and before I could really boot up my phone when I landed, Washington texted me to say welcome home. That made me smile because he was watching my flight to make sure I landed safely and I really dug that about him; he was such a tech guy.

When a man treats you like you are the only woman in the world, you don't mind giving up a little booty. I know some women who give it all and get nothing in return; I got it all and more. Now, you're probably wondering if this guy was so great what the heck could be wrong with him... well, honey, I am getting to it.

Now, I was in Georgia and he lived in Maryland. He decided to surprise me one day and drove so I wouldn't have to pick him up from the airport. I knew this was a test to see if I would have another man in the house. I wasn't stupid and he didn't have that problem from me. I was only interested in Washington; I would be a fool to try and play a man that gave me almost everything I ever wanted.

The doorbell rang early in the morning and it was him; I was so happy to see him that I hugged him and everything. As the day went on, we drank and ate and drank some more until I got a bit sick. The next day I was in bed, recovering from his homemade mojitos. He left to go to the store, but while parked in my driveway I noticed him sitting there on his cell and didn't really think much about it so I let it go. When he got back from the store, again he sat out in the driveway chatting on the cell and I brushed it off.

Washington came in, warmed me up some soup, and served it to me in bed. I thought I struck gold here, but then he had this look on his face and I asked what was wrong. He said, "Nothing, I just love you so much… I am feeling emotional right now." I leaned over and hugged him. *Wow!* I was thinking to myself. *He doesn't mind showing his feelings. Where has this man been all my life?* By this time we had been dating for a while and he wanted to close the long distance thing up by moving me to his home in Maryland. It took a lot of convincing me that it would work with all those folks in the house. Washington made way over $150k per year, but the minor detail he left out was that he was taking care of the entire family. That's why I was looked at as a threat: their meal ticket was about to fly the coop.

I'm flying the coop!

Chapter Eight

I lived in a big, beautiful house in Alpharetta, GA and had the deal of a lifetime to purchase it, but my ass will do almost anything for the sake of love. We decided I would move up to Maryland to his house that he shared with his family.

I am going to describe this damn house he lived in the best that I can: HOARDERVILLE! This man made over six figures and he lived in the basement of his own house *in a storage room,* and my dumb ass made six figures, lived with him, and brought my poor son and cat into the mess. I felt like I was in the real life Willy Wonka house! Ma and Pa took up two bedrooms upstairs and his fat ass sister took the other one. Now, if you could get through the garbage, diapers, and boxes, you might get downstairs, but watch it! The stair rails were loose and you might fall and never be seen again because there's so much junk in that damn house.

Downstairs to the left was the former storage area that we threw a futon mattress in and called our room. Right next door was a real bedroom his funky ass son occupied, and I do mean funky. If you were to continue to walk towards the light while kicking crap out of your way, you would find what might have been meant as a family room with an enormous weight bench that I used to hang my suits for work and a couch that, if you sat on it, you were sure to sink and never be seen or heard from again. There was a piano that I used as a shelf to store food because his fat ass sister wouldn't allow me to use the fucking kitchen. Then there was the fireplace that had stuff in it and in front of it so we couldn't enjoy that, either. There was so much crap down there it was a crying shame. Nonetheless, even being the neat freak that I am, I overlooked all that and moved in, putting my things in storage.

The agreement was for us to be at his house for 30 days and tell his fat sister to take over the house payments. Well, that never happened. 30, 60, and 90 days came and went, and every house that I picked out, this fool had a problem with. He acted as though he was moving out of a mansion or something! What a dumb-ass mother fucker!

Nonetheless, through all my tantrums, he didn't budge and then also told his sister all of our business. His sister didn't like me, nor did his mean mother; I didn't care because I hoped to be out of there soon, with or without his ass. His mother and sister used to call me voodoo girl because I burned incense and candles when in fact I was burning all that I could to kill the smell of shit diapers. I had to drink a lot just to get through that crazy household. I couldn't understand why our combined income was in the neighborhood of $260k a year and we lived like peasants. I really started to believe that this guy was just afraid to leave home or something. How could he even subject me to this crazy situation for this long? I was no better for staying for that long and believing his lies over and over again.

It turned out that this fool was cheating on me from the start and his reason was that I didn't listen to him about his day at work. So basically, because I didn't listen to him about his day, he went and fucked the next woman? So that was another issue on top of the hoarding I was exposed to. There was also the fact that when he went to work and I was left at the house, his family would gather at the top of the stairs to say mean things about me and he didn't have the balls to defend me. His sister seemed more like the girlfriend than I did; she got to spend his money and ruled the house like they were fucking.

Nothing I said made a damn difference in how he dealt with his family's treatment of me. The basement flooded one time and my cat was floating on a box like in a commercial and water was everywhere. In my mind I was saying good, now maybe we could throw some of this shit out! But nope, this idiot sat it out to dry then brought it back in. The bathroom toilet backed up and the laundry room was soaked in sewage; of course his fat ass sister blamed me because I use Charmin and they use that one-ply tissue! There were many issues on top of the hoarding situation. There came a time when my two older kids came to visit and my eldest son thought I was mad for living like that, and my daughter, who is very outspoken, said aloud, "Wow, what happened? This place looks like shit!" Of course his fat sister heard her, so she didn't like my mini-me, either... and I didn't care.

Well, the cheating and the fights continued for months and I got the message that he would never leave that house. So I started to make arrangements to move back to Georgia. Unfortunately, I was under this cat's roof Monday through Friday morning, but I left right after work to fly back to Atlanta to purchase food and pay the bills. My youngest son and my cat held down the house while I worked in Washington, D.C.

Getting back to idiot boy, who just happened to work for the White House (I'm sure when they read this book they're not going to like what I have to say about their precious employee). Well, idiot boy and I were still having relations, and all the while, he was still cheating with a co-worker before he secured his gig at the White House. This girl just happened to be the daughter of George Clinton (yes, Mr. Funkadelic Knee Deep and all that shit). His dumb ass was telling her all my business and I knew very little of hers (go figure). Anyway, she and I found each other on Facebook. I emailed her to ask her if she was seeing idiot boy or not and she said, "I'm sorry things didn't work out for you and so-and-so." I told her that was funny because I was still fucking his fat ass; she had the nerve to call me a slut when she was the one coming into my mix, not the other way around. I was puzzled about how she figured that one when I was still living there. Boy, he thought he was a player, thinking that he had two women fighting over him.

Well, I guess he didn't like that his bitch and I touched base and compared some notes before it got a little ugly, because idiot boy changed the combination to the front door and shipped my suits to my home in Georgia while I was already en route to Maryland to go to work the next day. How ugly was that? When I got to the house, of course he left his fat ass sister to do his dirty work and she was more than happy because I was a threat. She thought I was going to take her piggy bank away and she would actually have to go to work and pay a bill or two herself instead of using other people in the house that *did* work, namely me and idiot boy.

Well, the cops came because I had my new friend (I will get into that shortly) call the police and they came out and made comments like, "Oh damn, not her," and, "Damn that fat bitch." Those were the things that were being said about idiot boy's sister. The police felt my pain and asked where the man of the house was. I told them his punk ass was at work and left his sister to do his dirty work. The police were in shock, and if you can shock them, you're doing something.

Let me back it up a bit. I forgot to mention that, while I was home over the weekend in Georgia, he had me served by the Sherriff to not come to his job. I guess he feared that I was going to fuck his ass up for doing me wrong; what a sissy. He was evil enough to turn my cell phone off, too, which is why I will never go in on a family plan with someone I'm just dating again. Anyway, the police came and went, but before they left, they told me that I could go and have the locks changed if I wanted to because I received mail there. I had legal rights, but I didn't take them up on it because there would have been some bloodshed in that house and it wouldn't have been mine, that's for sure.

I went back to cell block H (for Hoarderville) with idiot boy and his family with a smile on my face. There was nothing they could say or do that night that could mess my mood up.

Moving on further to talk about my new friend, my black knight was more than happy to put me up for a few nights. He took me to get some clothes so I could go to work and make that money, honey. While I was at work, he was busy writing up everything that I needed to defend myself against idiot boy in court. Court day came, and of course, idiot boy backed down when he learned that he might lose his top security clearance if he continued. The White House didn't need that kind of attention, nor did the other government job he had at the time.

So, I walked into the courtroom dressed to the nines and put on my innocent face before the judge, and he wasn't immune to that look at all. I turned around and there was idiot boy. When our names were called, the judge took one look at the both of us in complete disbelief. Idiot boy informed the judge that he wanted to drop the restraining order, and that was the end of that crap for the time being, at least. I walked out and idiot boy circled me like a shark in the water. He came over to me and started to cry. I wasn't sure why since he's the one who thought he was mack daddy, listening to his single, no-life-having, fat ass sister.

So, my black knight was waiting in the car for me so we could drive back to Atlanta together, and all the while I knew in the back of my head that wasn't going to be the last time I saw idiot boy. One would think so after all that drama, but we had been together for a couple of horrible years, so I was kind of brainwashed, if you will.

While I was driving on our way back to Atlanta, I got pulled over in North Carolina for speeding. My black knight decided that he wanted to flex his legal knowledge again, and this time it almost got me arrested because it was a brother who pulled my ass over. I got a ticket for $245; I was pissed, but we kept on. It was the 4th of July and all of the police were out, so I behaved until we got to my house.

The next day, Black Knight and my youngest son went to the movies, and lo and behold, who showed up on my doorstep but idiot boy. I knew he wasn't finished making my life miserable. There he was, right there in that little green BMW that he inherited from his last girlfriend who passed away, all fat and sweaty and smiling; I couldn't let him in my house! Black Knight would have killed that man and probably me, too, for letting him in. Well, idiot boy stayed at a hotel near my home after I told him a little white lie that I had family visiting and they didn't want him in the house. He drove all the way back to Maryland, and in North Carolina, near where I was pulled over, so was he... I thought that was so funny.

Idiot boy was doing everything to try and win me back; sending flowers to my job in DC, calling, giving me money, and I took it because I needed it. Idiot boy tended to surface from time to time, asking for my hand in marriage after all that damn drama. Once I told him no and meant it, he backed off a bit but would still call to be noisy and see what I was doing. Well, I could tell that idiot boy found someone because he tended to get smart with me, just like it was when I was living with him and he met that damn broad, Kim, at his job.

Chapter Nine

Now, back to my new little friend who became my black knight in shining armor. I met him one day after working in DC; he chased my car down until I pulled over to talk to him. I needed a distraction because I was just headed back to what I called my prison cell at that house with idiot boy before the combination door change and all that drama.

This black knight was so dark, completely the opposite of what I normally like, but when he smiled and I found out he was in law school, I was instantly drawn to him. Did I mention those perfect white teeth and the pretty smile he had? Meanwhile, back in Atlanta, black knight was living in my house; but, soon after moving in, his jealous nature shone through. He started calling my associate, revealing my personal business, and showing up on her doorstep to discuss my relationship with idiot boy. So much energy was focused on me and what I was doing that black knight couldn't focus on getting a job. He was breaking into my emails and had me, idiot boy, and his girlfriend accusing one another of breaking into each other's emails. It was crazy!

No matter how many times I asked Black Knight, he denied it over and over again. It used to be a pleasure to leave DC on Fridays; I looked forward to going home to peace, and now I was regretting allowing this man into my home. All the chaos I had with him was worse than what I was dealing with before with idiot boy. Black Knight was doing everything from spying to going through my personal belongings; so much time was lost on his end for doing those things. Sunday came around and it was time to go back to DC. He made up some crazy reason for why he needed to go with me, so I drove back with him. Since I flew down, we drove his car back, and when we got back to DC, the rage grew and grew.

One night, while driving on a freeway up there, he decided to pull over on the freeway, got out of the car, walked over to my side, leaned in the window, and told me all of his personal documents were in the glove department. I was sitting there wondering what this drama queen would do next; this man walked out into the busy lanes trying to get hit by a car in front of me! How selfish is that, to commit suicide in front of another just to fuck their head up for the rest of their life? Well, as luck would have it, not one car was driving near where he was; that was funny because there were a bunch of cars when we drove up and now there weren't. God had plans for his crazy ass, that's for sure. Not *one car* on a DC freeway, wow!

So I got out of the car and told him to get his ass back in the car. That drama finally ended, but I wasn't in the clear; it rolled over to the room I was renting. This guy just couldn't handle alcohol; I just hated to see him with beer or wine. Every time this guy drank it was drama-ville. He accused my landlord of liking me and setting me up with people; I was like, wow, this guy is sick.

I tolerated this mess for a minute and we drove back to Atlanta, at my expense of course. All was quiet for a short while and then he started drinking, and I knew his pattern of ruining my peace while at home by then. True to fashion, he drank a 40-ounce beer and I counted down to drama. This man threw himself down my stairs at home, hit my cat on the way down, and I ran after the cat to make sure he was ok, not giving a damn about Black Knight and his fucked up self. He tried to say I pushed him, but I didn't; he said his shoulder was knocked out of place, but I doubt it was.

All I could think about is how to get this mother fucker out of my house. When I called the police it was useless because Black Knight would show his DC badge and they took his word for the reason why I called the police; they told us to get along and left, but not after looking at my wall of fame and asking, "Who are you? Are you somebody famous?" I just looked at the officer and asked if we could just get him out of my house and they said no. I can see why people get rid of their partners; I had such evil thoughts about this man.

So now I was stuck with someone living in my house that made threats towards me after I helped him get a job with a bodyguard friend of mine. I really thought this cat went crazy; the nutty look in his eyes was really scary, but I've been threatened by the best, so what he was bringing was just a headache.

Another incident that happened with him was during one of his tantrums. He decided to ask me if I wanted to be with him and I said no. He went downstairs, grabbed a knife, and acted as though he was going to stab himself! I tried to reach for the knife and ended up with a deep gash on my thumb. It was exhausting dealing with a man that acts like that! When he finally decided to move out, it was with another woman and I was relieved. She could deal with his shit!

Black Knight just couldn't leave me be; there was this mirror that he gave to me, but since I wasn't with him, he wanted it back. When I said I wouldn't because he gave it to me, he called the police again. So I gave him his damn mirror just so I could have some peace. Well, that wouldn't be the end of Black Knight; we're cool now just as long as he stays in his own space and leaves me alone.

One time I loaned him my son's car and he didn't come right back. When I drove to the corner after yelling on the phone for him to bring the damn car back, he came racing across the gas station parking lot, driving like some damn fool. I immediately grabbed the keys and lit into him about abusing my kindness; he tended to take advantage of that a lot. In my opinion, he just takes and takes.

Chapter Ten

Well, this other guy we will call Fireman met me online, and at the time, I was flying back and forth from DC to Atlanta. Fireman wanted to meet me, so I said ok, meet me at the Atlanta airport on Friday at 10 pm. As I was walking out of the airport, I got to the baggage claim area and waited for my date. Lo and behold, someone tapped me on my shoulder and I turned around in excitement, looking up… and then I looked down. Ah, damn he's a short one, literally speaking.

I looked at him and smiled to be kind, but I was pissed and had loads of questions, like how did he take those pictures that made him look tall? I wondered why I didn't ask him his freaking height. I was feeling pretty angry about the deception of it all, and I wondered what other surprises he had for me. I proceeded to walk toward the taxis that were out there. Fireman offered to take me home, but I said that's okay. I didn't want him to know where I lived so he could just pop in on me anytime he felt like it.

He had traits I personally don't like in a man; he was short and had a dark complexion; that's just my preference, so don't get mad at me. Needless to say, when he wanted to make a date to come and see me the next day, I was a no show. We spoke every now and then when I was bored, but that's pretty much it. His personality was very dry and I couldn't take having to hold the entire conversation on the phone; he was the type that just sat on the damn phone and didn't say anything. Well, that was Fireman... on to the next one.

Chapter Eleven

This next one came from a well-to-do, high-ranking family; his father rubbed shoulders with presidents and other high-ranking officials. That was the father; not much I can say about the little bastard I was dealing with. I will call this one Senator, and that's all I can say about him without coming up missing for spilling the beans.

This clown was a trip and a half. Senator had all that I thought I wanted. To be the wife of a state official was going to be different for me. Dressing differently than I like to and acting differently would have been overwhelming for me, but I was willing to do it so I allowed myself to get sucked into his world. This cat was the top dog of scam artists that I had ever been exposed to. He got me for $20,000, and the funny thing was that I didn't see it coming. Next thing I knew I was being introduced to mayors and other officials; I was a guest on his radio show and sat next to the mayor to talk about politics, something I have no interest in at all; but I did it for a love that was pretty much one-sided.

I paid for this and for that and was always told, "I will make sure you get all of this back when we win the election." Every time we went out to eat or entertain other officials, he would open his big mouth and say we would cover the bill, and it was sometimes $2,000.00 just to fucking eat dinner that wasn't good or even enough. I was flying back and forth paying for hotels, and I finally said enough when this fool wanted me to buy a black SUV with tinted windows. Senator was so bold with it that he would have dealerships calling me asking where I wanted the vehicle delivered to. My jaw was on the floor. But that wasn't the end of his spending spree; he picked out this huge house in Maryland near water and it had its own private boat dock, shed, and other top notch amenities that only well-to-do people could afford. News flash! I was not well-to-do; not yet, anyway.

I was really feeling overwhelmed and I wanted to be able to do these things, but I wasn't financially able to. He wanted a nice place where we could entertain his guests. Since I'd met a few of them, I could understand why he wanted to present a good front, but damn! Why not ask your rich daddy for the money instead of looking to me for everything?

Then came the time where he practically put me in charge of his campaign. He had all the confidence in the world that I could make calls and answer questions on his behalf, which I couldn't and wouldn't, but I did try to guide the staff and that was hard. Most of them had worked with some experienced people in politics and they could tell I didn't know what the fuck I was talking about. You could tell Senator was spoiled and used to having things go his way, but I wasn't used to being a flunky. I *had* flunkies; not the other way around.

I was a frequent guest on his show and later I knew why. It wasn't because he was so damn in love with me; it was because his male audience loved my looks and voice. I later found out that I received fan mail. Senator loved the attention I was able to draw to him from others who would come to him just to have an opportunity to speak to me. He was so focused on his campaign that he was not able to love or show any kind of affection toward me. When he would call me it was to ask questions, write some legal document for him, or fire a staff member, and he would always call late at night with no consideration for my rest, and even at that time it was to get information.

I don't know if he knew how old I was because he wanted me to have children and I looked at him crazy because mine are grown. What the fuck do I look like? I'm not doing that again, fool! I didn't say that, but I felt like it.

I had a blog talk radio show during our time together with a huge following around the world, and the great Senator thought he had a way to reach others and, most importantly, reach my circle of friends and family. Boy, that was embarrassing because he would get on my show and just try to take over, not to mention his voice sounded like he was gay and people would call me up and ask me who the gay dude on my show was. I would often defend him, but in the back of my mind I wasn't happy about it. Hell, Mr. Rogers has a deeper voice than this man. Well, Mr. Senator wanted this and that, and the straw that broke that camel's back (as if the previous stuff wasn't enough) was that he knew I was in town for a couple of days, and when I called to tell him after driving all the way up from Georgia, he told me he was busy. Oh really, Mr. Senator? Busy, eh? He must have found a new sucker because by this time I had cut him down so low with funds he was barely making any kind of profit on me. So, I got mad and felt that was my chance to let him have it, everything that I had been holding in for months from the start of our relationship.

Senator was so bold, in fact, that he stored my rich friends' and relatives' numbers in his phone and would call them up to ask for donations for his dumb ass campaign. It got so bad that I had to seek the services of my legal eagle, Black Knight, who was eager to oblige because he still carried a torch for me, and I knew that if anyone messed with me he would go after them with all that he had in him to give. Although Black Knight was trouble, he was hell when it came to the legal system. After a few cease and desist letters, Senator finally gave up his harassing calls to my family and friends. He tried to befriend me on a popular job site; naturally, I declined, and that's the end of that fool.

Chapter Twelve

Although this next cat actually came later, I have to tell you about him now; I will call him Yellow and Black because of the well-known restaurant he ran in Atlanta, Georgia.

Well, things started off hot and heavy. I met him at a cool Italian restaurant in Atlanta at 9pm, and I am a real stickler for being on time; I feel if I respect your time, you should respect mine, but he was a few minutes late. I was a bit perturbed but let it slide so we could eat and drink. His being slightly shorter than me took me aback, but his looks were similar to Harry Belafonte, which is what drew me to him.

Before I left for the evening, he asked if he could see me again and we met up again the very next day. Pretty soon, I was at his house every single day; I even had a key and was put on his flight plan with a southern airline. Things were moving fast, and to be honest, once I found out about his sign I had reservations. I have never liked Virgos and wondered when he was going to do something to piss me off; eventually, he did. He told me he was going to be at my house but showed up hours later – not minutes, but hours – and I was heated. Or when I would go to his house, which took me a good 45 minutes to get there depending on traffic, and he wasn't there. Or when he would say he was on his way and I was left waiting in my car and didn't want to go into his house without him there.

Black and Yellow worked like a beast; so much so that there was no way he could have a healthy relationship with any woman. I was just die-hard so I stuck around. When I expressed my concern about spending time together, he told me I was opinionated and no one could live up to my expectations. I didn't understand how that had anything to do with spending time together. He went on to say things about not being rich or famous like my past boyfriends. I couldn't believe how he flipped out on me; it was crazy, that's for sure.

I pretended I was cool with things after making up, but by this time red flags were up about this cat. It seemed to me that he only wanted to fuck something pretty; he even flew me down to meet his mother using his buddy pass. While down there with his mother, he showed no affection at all; he didn't hold my hand or anything. As a matter of fact, he walked ahead of me and acted as if I was a friend and not his woman. I never understood why he took me there. It just didn't make sense to me at all, but I let it go.

On the flight back, this asshole asked me if I was a member of the mile high club, I said no and then there was silence. I knew it was just a matter of time before he had to tell me, so he did. This dumb man sat there and told me how a woman was in the bathroom with her legs open and he accidently walked in, said sorry, closed the door, then turned around and went back and fucked her without knowing her name. I sat there in total disbelief. What was the point of him telling me that? After that there was a chill in the air and it was coming from me. I was becoming more and more turned off by this guy.

There were many more fights, but this one was wild. We had a fight in his house and I sat there again while he went off like a woman. Frustrated, I just got up and went to take a shower, thinking I was going to go home and never speak to this fool again. While I was in the shower, he knocked on the shower door to ask if he could join me and I said yes, thinking he was coming in to make up. I was shampooing my hair when he came in and I felt something by my ankles that was furry. I rinsed my hair so I could see what was going on, and this mother fucker brought his fucking tiny dog into the shower with us! The shower was barley big enough for one, never mind two and a damn dog. I stood there in shock while this dumb fuck proceeded to shampoo the dog in the shower with us! So instead of trying to make up with me, he brought his damn dog in the shower, shampooed her, and pampered her while I was standing there. I just couldn't believe what was going on! I got the hell out of the shower, feeling filthier than when I went in because of the fur from the dog.

This cheap fuck offered to take me out, but wanted me to drive all the time. He never once offered to put gas in my car, and he felt that he paid for everything because he bought a handful of dinners. I really paid for a lot because of the back and forth from my house to his and driving him around because he always said he didn't have gas in his car. The endless issues with this cat drove me crazy; he was such a handful.

The last encounter with him was when I brought up not spending time together again and he said I hurt his feelings. He went on to say how he couldn't live up to my expectations and asked who made me the relationship expert. I knew I wanted to end this crazy cycle with him at that point. So I wrote an email, and of course, I got a nasty one back; I really didn't care by this point. Any feelings I had for him had faded and I was so ready to move on. Black and Yellow kept me on his companion list until I flew up to NYC to see my daughter. I must say, I was very nervous that he would cut me off and I would be stuck in NYC with no way back to Atlanta. Black and Yellow didn't, though, and my trip was good up until a crazy storm came out of nowhere. I knew upon my arrival in Atlanta that I was going to be greeted by the self-proclaimed Coffee King.

Chapter Thirteen

Upon my return, I met up with my new friend who's in a multi-level marketing company. I met him on a very popular online dating site. This guy started off kind of strange, flashing his fancy cars and home and coming off as only wanting to talk about himself. That was a turn off to me, but I thought what the heck, let's see what this guy has going on besides his so-called wealth and self-proclaimed fame. I couldn't believe he actually thought I heard of him before. Why would I have? I wasn't into multi-level marketing like that; the twist was that my first-born's father was and he knew of this man.

We met at the airport after my visit with my daughter in New York. He waited for me while I went to get my car and followed behind his hired driver to his lovely home in Buckhead. I must admit I was impressed; I have seen bigger and better, but he walked like a cat that brought home a mouse. As I walked in, two of his daughters came running down the stairs to greet him and then they saw me peering over his shoulder. The look those girls gave me were kind of mixed, like *damn, another one* and *damn, I wanted my daddy to myself this weekend.*

All four of us went out to dinner, which was kind of weird for a first date, but I went with the flow. I really didn't understand these men not courting in a proper manner; nonetheless I had an ok time. When we finished dinner and went back to his house, the girls went upstairs and we went down to neck like high school kids. I saw a soft side of this man that I had hoped would be out for me all the time. It was getting late and I was sent home like child; I felt kind of strange about that. The girls weren't exactly five years old; I wasn't sure why we were hiding like we were doing a bad thing.

There's definitely a difference in the men on the west coast and the east coast, that's for sure. The men on the west coast that I have dealt with always take you out and court you the right way; the ones on the east coast are cheap and act strange. That was Saturday with the self-proclaimed coffee king.

Monday came and I checked my email, and sure enough, little man Black and Yellow wrote me a Dear John letter. I thought that was so funny because I thought we were a done deal; that day we had words with each other. That man acted too much like a bitch for me to continue to deal with. Black and Yellow's letter was insulting. I sat on it for a minute and then decided to write back and let him know what's really going on, so here's what I had to say in my email: "I thought we were a done deal that particular day of the incident and I met someone, so no need to email me back." I am sure he didn't like that, but oh well, that's life.

Chapter Fourteen

This next nut is the latest and the absolute last (I hope); I will call this one Grocery since I met him in the grocery store near my place of employment. This guy appeared to have it all together, on the outside at least. There he stood with his white shoes without a single nick on them and his sky blue shirt and white shorts, looking like he just got off a cruise ship. I gave him my number and he called me to meet; I invited him to my house because I just wasn't in the mood to meet in a public place and my tire was recently repaired.

So, Grocery came by my home and sat down, running his mouth: "I've been all around the world 20 times." I sat there in amazement and total disbelief. You can't just tell me anything; I've been around some good liars in my time. This guy was a big mouth liar and so I got fed up and told him to hold his horses. Of course he was offended, but I really didn't give a damn. He had the nerve to sit on my couch and act as though he'd never seen a cell phone, iPad, iPhone, etc. I wondered where the hell he'd been; even folks in the desert know about these things.

I wanted some entertainment, so I listened to this cat go on and on about how he spent $100k to travel and places he had been to that he couldn't even pronounce. I thought that was funny; I had to laugh out loud. This man seemed like he was straight from the backwoods of somewhere when he said, "worser." I just about fainted. I started to wonder what his educational background was because his vocabulary was ridiculous. How the heck are you Mr.

International when you can't pronounce a country's name or remember the culture or foods?

Now, all this guy did was call me and insist that he wanted a relationship with me. I said, "You have to get to know me first, right? You may not like me as of this minute and I don't really like your ass. You cannot force me to be with you!" This guy was a real piece of work indeed. The other day while I was at work, I texted him to move on and to stop calling me for the third time, and of course his response was that he needed me in his life and to stop being difficult. The way this fool was acting you would have thought I laid it down on his ass or something.

I still can't get over him driving a Saturn that nobody drives anymore, an old and beat up piece of shit, green with chipped paint... what an insult to think I was going to fall for his bullshit. I was bored and played with him like a cat until I got distracted again, which was quickly due to his lack of ability to effectively communicate with me. That just drove me nuts.

Well, for the final bang with this fool, I reluctantly agreed to have lunch with him. While we were there I was wondering why he was scruffy and disheveled. He looked very different from when I saw him at the grocery store. I rushed through my food so I could leave and get back to work. I politely asked for a to-go box and he sat across from me looking into his cheap ass phone like it had all kinds of features. The signs were all there.

I said I had to get back to work and thank you for lunch. As we walked out, he walked me to my car and kind of walked fast to his car. I was pulling out and the waiter came running out saying, "Hey! Hey, someone has to pay for this bill!" I looked over at that bubble-eyed bastard and said, "Hey, aren't you going to pay?" He said, "No!" I couldn't believe what was happening to me. This bastard came up here without money and never intended to pay for lunch. Thank God I had money to pay.

When I walked in, the two waiters were laughing. I found it kind of humorous as well, but I was more embarrassed than anything. Both waiters were young men and the white one asked me if I wanted him to beat his ass. I told him I really didn't know him, so it was cool. Even the young waiter was saying that was fucked up and he needed his ass beat. Now, that's a shame when a kid is saying that about an older man and it's true.

I asked the black waiter why did he ran to my car and he said, "Because your car is nicer and I figured you had the money." My jaw fell to the ground. Well, ladies, let that be a lesson to you to always make sure you have money when going out on dates these days! Courtship seems to be a thing of the past.

The dirty south has not been kind to me; not one bit. It's so bad that when I come to work, men and women want to know who am I dating and how is the relationship going. Let's say it's been rough, but very entertaining at my expense. I hope this comes across the way I tell the story to friends, co-workers, and others because they laugh and laugh till they start crying. I started to feel like the comic! Hell, I have enough material, that's for sure. I find my life kind of funny, too; I guess that's why I share my stories. Then again, it's kind of sad that I am truly longing to be with a good man. It just hasn't been in the cards for me.

Chapter Fifteen

While visiting family in Greenville, South Carolina, my niece was in tears laughing about my romantic comedy dating experiences. She was talking to another person about it and wanted me to tell it in my own words. It was funny how she remembered all the details, some of which I've even forgotten. I was reminded of a couple that I forgot. One we'll call Long Beach, since that's where he lived.

He was very handsome, tall, and sharp; *What could be wrong with this one?* I wondered. I would soon find out. Long Beach flew me from Atlanta to LA to visit him, and I had to wonder how a wealthy man lived in a trailer park. It was nice, but still a freaking trailer park. I then wondered why everything in the house was broken, at least everything that had glass once like a fish tank stand without a fish tank, the stove glass door, and even the refrigerator glass shelves were broken. I thought, *Dang, some woman was really pissed off up in here.* I asked Long Beach about it, and he told me about the woman that went off on him, taking a bat and breaking everything in the house. I felt strange being in that house because I wasn't sure if the psycho woman would return or not, but Long Beach reassured me that his house was safe, so I let it go.

Once he showed me around the house I relaxed a bit but noticed that the house was smaller than I'd thought. I walked to the master bedroom and it was pretty nice; cramped, but nice. I walked into the bathroom and this man didn't even take the time to remove the previous woman's stuff. I thought oh well; let me make use of it, after all, hair products are not cheap. I wanted to take a shower and relax.

Stepping into the shower was horrible. It was filthy; there was caked up dirt on the floor and tile. When I asked Long Beach about it, he said that he just threw Comet on the floor and used his foot to clean, but that couldn't be the case. That shower floor was horrible to the point of being black. I didn't want to touch a thing in there, yuck!

That's not the worst part. The part where people laugh is when I describe how this man didn't mention that he wore a urostomy bag for his bowels. I tried not to stare at it, but it did bother me somewhat because I didn't know what it was for. Long Beach was very smart about how to make love to me without me even knowing about that bag. First he kept his shirt on and he would never lay on top of me; that in and of itself was odd.

Long Beach had many issues; one was his lack of grooming himself. His toe nails were so long they were curved, discolored, and smelled, not to mention his smoking sucked, too, but at least he took it outside out of respect for me. I lost a lot of weight living with him for that long two weeks because I didn't want to eat anything in that house. I was scared to touch anything in there, so I starved myself most of the time.

I drove his car around town, but I was often low on money so I didn't buy anything to eat until I was at the breaking point. Long Beach was complaining about my weight, saying he wasn't attracted to me anymore. I was 5'9" and 165 pounds at the time and *he* wasn't attracted to *me*? With all of his issues he should have been glad that I was even dealing with this fucked up shit. I had an interview with Yahoo, but Long Beach thought it would be best if I went back to Atlanta. I went back with a smile on my face just because I was getting away from his nasty house. Goodbye, Long Beach, and good riddance!

Conclusion

I just received a call from the self-proclaimed Atlanta coffee king. He called to tell me he apologizes for how things ended between the two of us. I really don't know why he called; at this point I could care less. I guess he needed to call me to make himself feel better… after weeks of not hearing from all of these fools.

I moved on with my life and married a wonderful man; no sooner than we tied the knot, most of these fools mentioned above came right back straight out of the woodwork. I find it funny how they have the nerve to be upset with me for getting married when they weren't around. I guess they wanted me to sit and wait until they decided to call or text me.

Internet dating sites have been around for some time now, and I am sure I left a few good stories out because most of them are more embarrassing than the ones I have mentioned here. I might have buried those so far in the back of my brain to avoid traumatizing anybody, most of all myself. I sure hope the few stories I shared with you have made you laugh! The next book is *Deceived (You Can't Make This Up)*, and the drama continues.

About the Author

ChaCha McKnight is a native Californian and former model, dancer, and performing artist who has worked in a corporate environment after putting her love for the entertainment business on the back burner to raise her three children, Valentino, Tatiana, and Lorenzo. She now resides in San Jose, CA and enjoys playing with her cat, PooPoo, and traveling to Puerto Rico and other surrounding islands. Her email address is chachamcknight@gmail.com.

www.ingramcontent.com/pod-product-compliance
Lightning Source LLC
Chambersburg PA
CBHW060953040426
42445CB00011B/1137